CW81845777

FIRST AID FOR HANGOVERS

Written by Rob Alcraft
Illustrated by Scruffy Pup

KUDOS

Published by Kudos, an imprint of Top That! publishing plc
Copyright © 2005 Top That! Publishing plc
Tide Mill Way, Woodbridge, Suffolk, IP12 IAP, UK.
www.kudosbooks.com
Kudos is a trademark of Top That! Publishing plc
All rights reserved

CONTENTS

The Morning After	3	Sugar Rush Treatment	30
Know your Enemy	4	Vitamin Vitals	32
Preventing Hangovers	10	Pain Potions	34
Cures for the Morning After	20	Sex Therapy	36
		Boil in the Bag	38
Go Back to Bed (aka The Churchill)	22	Hair of the Dog	40
The Hero's Water & Air Cure	24	Bloody Mary	42
Cola Doctor	26	Prairie Oyster	44
The Greasy Cafe Breakfast	28	Banana Cow	46
		Feeling Better?	48

THE **MORNING** *after...*

Feeling hungover? As though your visual cortex is being blow torched? Like someone's inside your head, beating it about with a stick? And down in the dark of your insides do you feel that ominous ache, as an endless stream of toxins go round your screaming body? Are you feeling that at any moment an evacuation of your bowels will be necessary, possibly back up through your mouth? It's the price we all pay for over-indulging in Satan's brew, that only a few hours ago seemed so tempting and all powerful and good... but never fear, help is at hand...
Once you've read the book use the dice, one for while you're out and one for the morning after, to help you with those difficult decisions or just grab the glass and down another.

know your ENEMY

Why do you feel so bad? Unfortunately for you, the answer isn't as simple as you'd like it to be. But let's start with the basics: you're suffering from an overdose of a poisonous, depressive drug. Let's just run through those symptoms, shall we (even though you may already be intimately acquainted with them)?

IT'S all in your **HEAD**

The fun you think you had last night was alcohol working its wicked way through your soft pulpy brain. It works first on the nerve cells, interfering with their communication. Your cerebral cortex (your You) is the first to be affected; you may get euphoric, and you may ramble pointlessly.

Alternatively, you may fall victim to exaggerated emotional states, get into fights or snog people you don't like – maybe a combination of all of those things.

Keep drinking and you can look forward, medically speaking, to stupor, vomiting, incontinence, coma and possibly death from respiratory arrest.

TOO sexy for your **BRAIN**

At about the same time as you start to talk nonsense, there's a lump of your brain called your hypothalamus which, under the influence of alcohol, suddenly kicks your sex drive into gear. You become an amorous but dribbling drunk person.

You're not remotely sexy – but you don't know that.

Meanwhile your pituitary gland is also having a party. It's normal secretions that send orders to your kidneys to reabsorb water go haywire, and you have to spend more and more of your evening urinating – although as things get worse this may not be the only thing you'll be doing in the toilet; just don't hug the bowl too tightly.

Your body, under the influence of alcohol and the various chemicals that come with it, is, in hangover terms, going into self-destruct mode. But that's not the half of it.

YOUR body's AGONY

A quick tour round your body's agony should be instructive at this point.

Let's start with a look up your urinary tract shall we? That heavy night's drinking and all that urinating triggered by your confused kidneys means you're heavily dehydrated. All of your organs have shrunk. Even your brain.

Your brain, clever thing, can't feel pain, but as it shrinks due to water loss the pain-sensitive filaments that tie it inside your skull are stretching, and you get one hell of a headache.

Another consequence of your binge has been to flush your system of some of its most important salts, vitamins and nutrients.

Nifty things, such as potassium, that your muscles and nerves need to function have been washed out into the pub toilet.

Other chemical effects of alcohol mean you are also vitamin A, B and C deficient. Well done. You feel nausea, fatigue and even more headache. (That quickly downed drink doesn't seem like such a good idea now does it?)

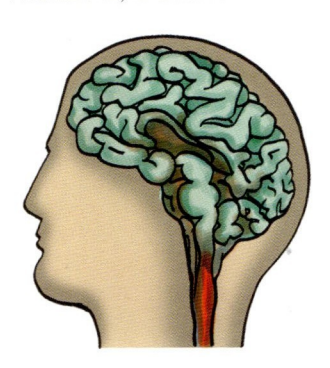

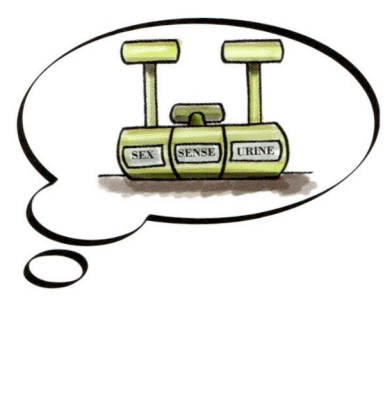

Liver PUNISHMENT

It's your liver's job to destroy poisons, and all night it's been at work disposing of ethanol alcohol.

However, this produces its own nasty, toxic by-products, among them acetaldehyde. Don't worry if you can't say it because this is, in fact, an unspeakable poison that helps cause yet more nausea, fatigue and, you guessed it, headache.

On top of all this, alcohol has also given your body's store of glycogen a good kicking. This important source of energy is kept in the liver, but under the influence of alcohol is converted into glucose and, you guessed it, flushed down the toilet. This explains that weak, "I-will-fall-over" feeling that most people know only too well.

With your body experiencing this onslaught it's time to get some help.

preventing HANGOVERS

In far flung parts of the Caribbean, drinkers used to try and avoid hangovers by rubbing a lemon under their drinking arm. Try this if you like, but there are a other few things you should know first about preventing hangovers.

10

BEWARE **Blubber**

The hangover you get will depend not just on how much you drink, but on how big you are, how fit you are, and how much blubber you're carrying around.

So if you're a little wisp of a thing don't think you can drink as much as a monster-sized boy. Similarly, you girls can't drink as much because you are saddled with more body fat as a percentage of your body weight. However, this does mean you can survive a few minutes longer in the icy waters of the Atlantic before succumbing to exposure, because your blood flow is better insulated.

In 'drinking terms' though fat is bad news. Fatty tissues don't hold much water, and won't absorb much alcohol. More of what you drink ends up in your blood stream and you will suffer accordingly.

And one more thing, smoking will multiply your hangover tenfold. Smoke less, and you can drink more but then you'd be undoing the good of smoking less – the choice is yours but remember, poisons, whether alcohol or nicotine, equal sickness.

SAVE yourself PAIN

To save yourself some pain, learn to spit out anything cheap and nasty posing as a drink: just don't let it anywhere near your liver.

Why? Because drinks don't just contain ethanol – a relatively clean kind of alcohol that gets you drunk. They also pack a cocktail of chemicals of varying degrees of nastiness.

Some of them taste nice, and some get you drunk. Others just make you sick, and are only there because the people who made the drink don't know any better, or couldn't be bothered to find something else to flavour their drink with.

Here are a few simple rules to follow:

- **Don't drink cheap booze** – cheap red wine and whisky, for instance, often contain methanol, a fuel-type alcohol cousin of ethanol that will give you a hangover from hell. All cheap drinks will pack a whole load of chemicals and preservatives that will punish you the next morning.

• **Alcopop drinks** – drinks marketed at the 'yoof' market, are typically fizzy and full of sugar. You'll absorb the alcohol from fizzy drinks faster, which is fine, but the sugar will speed up the depletion of your vitamin B – making your hangovers worse.

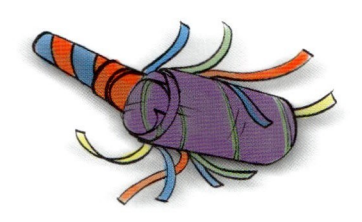

• **Don't mix drinks** – mixing drinks means multiplying your hangover symptoms, so don't.

13

- **Drink slower**, and go for lower alcohol content – give your body the chance to cope.

- **Drink water** – if you must insist in doing any or all of the above, try to squeeze in a glass or two of water during your drinking session.

- **Line your stomach** – Protecting your vitals is the key when you know you have a heavy night ahead of you. Ideally, eating a meal before you begin drinking is the best option – this means that the alcohol is absorbed more slowly, and your body has a better chance of dealing with the excess as the evening progresses.

If you know you'll be starting to drink before you get a chance to eat properly then you need to line your stomach.

Just a glass of milk or a lump of cheese – or even a tablespoonful of oil – when consumed before the first drop of alcohol can be the difference between happy drinking and the headache from hell.

PIGGING Out

One of the most effective and, let's face it, most pleasing ways to avoid a hangover is to eat.

A late night pig out is not only good for your hangover, it is to be recommended to all drunk people. In fact all sorts of food at all sorts of times during a night out is a very good idea. Food works to fight your hangover by increasing your metabolism. It activates alcohol absorption and increases the speed at which your body processes alcohol. By the time you go to bed, who knows what you might have saved yourself?

Pizza and pasta are a particularly good idea, since they're a source of carbohydrates and usually come with lots of cheese, and that means amino acids, which your stomach is craving. But any food you can keep down is probably a good idea – the more vitamins and nutrients you can reintroduce into your system the better you are going to feel in the morning.

If you're supposed to be watching your waist line, well, let's face it you've already fallen off the diet wagon with all that booze!

PURGE **Prevention**

This prevention method isn't one for the faint hearted, and like most quack remedies is a cure that can be worse than the illness. It's also completely unscientific. But hey, that sort of nicety didn't bother you when you started drinking, did it?

The 'up chuck' or throwing up method works on the amateur stomach pump principle. Rather than waiting for all the alcohol in your stomach to fizz through your liver, making you feel like death why not just get the stuff out?

Making yourself sick when you're very drunk is actually quite easy, and a lot more pleasantly forgettable than first thing in the morning on the bus to work. The essential tools of the operation are two waggling fingers applied to the back of the throat, and a friendly toilet to hug.

When you've been as sick as you can, you'll have the satisfaction that, not only can it not get much worse, but that some of the alcohol that was waiting to hammer your liver is now down the toilet.

This method should of course be used in conjunction with rehydration, teeth cleaning, and bed.

DRINK water

To avoid a hangover one of the most important things you have to do is put some water back into your system. Remember, those kidneys of yours have allowed your bladder to fill up like some crazed urinal, and you are now horribly dehydrated.

So drink three or four pints of water before going to bed. If you can fit it into your hectic schedule of body punishment, why not have a few glasses of water as you go through the evening?

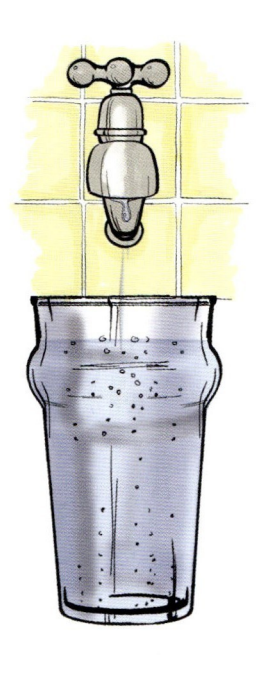

Of course this tried and tested method has one unfortunate side effect. You may indeed wake up in the night with a bladder the size of a football, but this, as we all know, is a lot easier to handle than a hangover.

So drink water. Don't wait until the morning; do it now. Oh, and if you do get up in the night, you may as well refill your bladder with even more H_2O – it couldn't hurt.

Cures for *the* MORNING AFTER

Even with all that good advice you're sure to lapse into your old drunken ways, so what can you do when you're feeling like death warmed up the morning (or afternoon) after?

Just be thankful you don't live in ancient Greece, where you'd now be chewing raw cabbage leaves – or for that matter Victorian England – there you'd find yourself gagging on a soot-filled milkshake. Ancient Romans enjoyed their cabbage too but while wearing a necklace of parsley and consuming two eels suffocated in wine!

Try the ancient ways if you like, but there are some new and better ideas that might just be able to save you, or at the very least shove you along the road to recovery.

Unpleasantness	low (this is easy)
Does it work?	effective delaying tactic
Ease index	almost no action required
Just say	"leave me alone, I'm going to die"

Go back to *bed* (aka The Churchill)

One sure way to combat hangover lethargy is to give in, and simply never get out of bed.

The beautiful, lethargic poetry of the stay-in-bed method was perfected by Winston Churchill who, as well as winning the Second World War, also enjoyed a drink. His favoured hangover strategy was to stay where he woke up, and have the newspapers brought up by his butler, along with a snifter of brandy or whisky to smooth off any rough edges to the early morning.

Churchill applied the stay in bed method rigorously – to the extent that when he dropped his newspaper the butler would have to come back and pick it up. Pursue this technique with equal dedication and you'll be rewarded with eventual victory. One dedicated servant will, however, be required. Alternatively, drag yourself out of bed briefly to stockpile suitable snacks, beverages and of course the remote control.

Unpleasantness .... high (unpleasant to mildly unbearable)

Does it work? .... yes, I'm afraid so

Ease index .... extreme willpower required

Just say .... "I'm going out, I may be some time"

the HERO'S water & air cure

When you went to bed last night you were around 90% water.

And that is how your body likes it. But, as we've already seen, your body, and kidneys in particular, have been taking the piss.

You now contain less water than you did, and you have to do something about it – pronto. So drink water, lots of it. Water will help your body recover.

After the water you need to expose yourself to some fresh air – don't whine, just do it.

The fresh air and exercise are an all round good thing for your body right now. The increased oxygen flow will help speed up your metabolic rate, and allow you to break down the alcohol and other poisons that are still fizzing through your system.

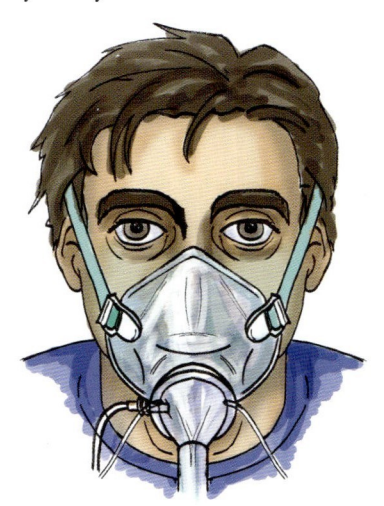

Unpleasantness .... medium (could cause irritation and retching)

Does it work? .... it helps early stage recovery

Ease index .... there are harder things

Just say .... "I'm gonna teach the world to sing in perfect harmony"

COLA doctor

One of the unfortunate effects of alcohol on the body is to irritate not just your friends (if they still are) but the linings of your stomach and intestine – a primary cause of vomiting and stomach pain in the hungover body.

So, assuming you don't have the equipment for a saline drip, or indeed kidney dialysis, cola is the next best thing to put back into your stomach. It will stay down when little else will – feeding your body with life-saving water and sugar. For any stomach-turning kind of hangover, this should be your first stage treatment.

Also consider sports drinks – designed to replace some of those sugars and salts sweated out on the field of play, but pretty good for replacing lost hangover salts too. If you can't handle the fizz, just shake the drink till it goes flat. And for the truly health aware, turn to fruit juice.

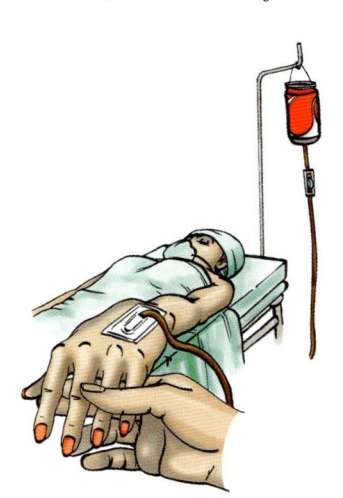

Unpleasantness ....medium (could induce vomiting)

Does it work?..surprisingly, yes

Ease index...................................if you can walk upright, you can benefit

Just say ...."full English, please"

the GREASY CAFE *breakfast*

This is a scientifically proven pig-out that works, reaching parts of your body that only greasy, wriggly fried things can reach.

The very act of getting up and walking to the café is the beginning of your cure, though what really counts is what you eat when you get there.

You need to order a full English breakfast. There must be tomatoes and eggs – which are the real magic foods. Egg yolk is rich in cysteine which, among other functions, is known to assist the processing of acetaldehyde – the evil toxic chemical that your liver produces from alcohol. Similarly tomatoes contain some of the vitamins you need, including vitamin C.

If at the end of your breakfast there's room, finish off with a banana. Monkeys know what they're doing – this curvy yellow fruit has sugar in the form of fructose, as well as potassium and magnesium. These are all things that your body really needs.

Unpleasantness	low (even you can handle it)
Does it work?	it'll stop you fainting
Ease index	you'll manage it
Just say	"I think I need to replenish my glycogen"

sugar *RUSH* treatment

When you're drinking you should avoid sugar like someone else's spit.

Sugar accelerates the depletion of your vitamin B supplies, and speedily sends you to the hangover from hell. Come the morning things have changed. Now you feel flaky and weak, and sugar is what you need. This is partly because alcohol has attacked your body's supply of glycogen, which you store in your liver. As a result of your alcohol binge this glycogen has been broken down into glucose, and flushed out with your urine.

The best way to replace lost sugar is with fruit juice or a banana. These contain fructose, which is the best sort of sugar for a hangover. But hey, if it has to be chocolate or sherbet lemons it will still help combat that wobbly new-born giraffe feeling common to people in your situation.

Unpleasantness	high (this is costly)
Does it work?	it can aid recovery
Ease index	do you have any money left from last night?
Just say	"give me a bottle of your most expensive vitamins please"

vitamin **vitals**

By now you should be completely aware that excessive amounts of alcohol will vent from your system just about every precious vitamin and mineral known to man.

Your brain, muscles, nerves, liver and a host of quite innocent membranes and soft fleshy bits have basically been robbed of things essential to their proper function. No wonder you feel as bad as you do.

You need to put the vitamin vitals back into your system.

Start with vitamins A, Bs of all sorts (especially B6) and C. While you're there chuck in cysteine, fructose, sodium and potassium. All these can be sourced from such delights as raw cabbage and runny eggs, but if you can't face these stick to vitamin tablets and try some of the other methods.

Unpleasantness	medium to dangerous
Does it work?	it can help
Ease index	just swallow
Just say	"my head, my head"

PAIN *potions*

With a bad hangover it may be tempting to swallow anything you think will make you feel better. You may even, in a drunken attempt to ward off tomorrow's evil hangover, find yourself popping some headache pills before you go to bed… big mistake…

Any painkiller mixed with alcohol will massively increase the damage done to your liver, and how bad you feel. The same goes for the next morning: avoid paracetamol and anything that has acetaminophen on the label. If you have to take a headache pill it needs to be the ibuprofen kind, otherwise you're just magnifying the damage already done to your poor put-upon liver.

If you really want to take some medication to cure your ailments there are plenty to choose from over your pharmacist's counter.

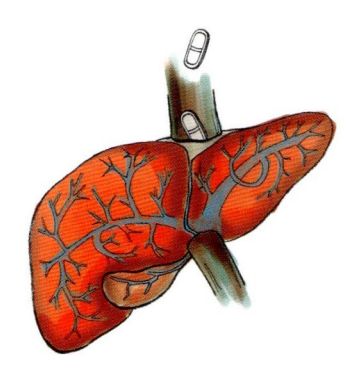

A favourite from Russia, now sold elsewhere as RU-21, is known as the KGB pill, supposedly because it was designed to help spies keep a clear head while drinking. It might help you avoid torture.

Unpleasantness	low (this could be pretty enjoyable)
Does it work?	who cares?
Ease index	that really depends, doesn't it?
Just say	"let's get jiggy"

SEX therapy

Wipe that sick from your face and turn towards that soft fleshy person who is sharing your hangover bed. They can make you feel better, in fact you can help each other…

Try to devise something vigorous and fairly sweaty, and if it includes massage, that's good. The longer it takes the better. You should feel the toxic weight lifting from your brain, and remember why you're alive in the first place.

If you haven't got anyone to have sex with, you need to find some other form of exercise. That's right, running, swimming, the gym – that sort of thing. It all works in very nearly the same way, increasing the oxygen flow to you brain and muscles, speeding up your metabolism and generally giving your body something better to do than whinge on about your hangover.

Unpleasantness	actually pretty nice
Does it work?	boiled vegetables don't moan
Ease index	tap-turningly easy
Just say	"I like it hot, hot, hot"

BOIL in the BAG

The Romans knew the value of a good hot bath, and who are we to argue? Plus this hot bath cure has a very low activity input – so basically you just have to lie there, which in the throws of a bad hangover, is probably all you can manage. Now that sounds pretty good, doesn't it?

This hot bath treatment works on the same principle as slowly boiling a lobster. They never make much protest, and in just the same way when you've warmed up sufficiently, your death-like hangover really won't seem so bad. Your aching muscles will slowly sooth, and your headache dissipates. You'll also sweat out some of those toxins which are hammering your system – and that, as you know, is a good thing.

This is an excellent combination cure, and should be applied with lots of water to drink, and perhaps a Bloody Mary (see page 42) perched on the side of the bath. If you don't have a bath, try a hot shower applied forcefully to the back of the head – it does wonders for a headache and muscle tension.

Unpleasantness..low to good

Does it work?...short term, yes.
Long-term, hopeless

Ease index..do you have an arm?

Just say.........................."I like tomato juice very much"

hair of the DOG

The hair of the dog idea comes from the folk remedy of treating dog bites with hair from the offending animal – but in this case there are no dogs or hair involved – you just drink some more alcohol, yes more alcohol.

And it works – basically by re-poisoning your liver and effectively bludgeoning your sickly organ into submission so that it doesn't bother you any more. Not for the sort of people who like counting their alcohol units, but that obviously isn't you.

The following three hair of the dog favourites also have the added benefit of containing some of the lost vitamins and nutrients your body craves (a clue perhaps to their enduring popularity and fame). Really this is an all round good thing, unless of course your job is operating some sort of limb-endangering machinery, in which case you'd probably be wise to think twice before employing this kind of cure.

BLOODY MARY

Reputedly invented in the roaring twenties by flapper-type people, the Bloody Mary has a chillingly healthy feel – and contains vodka, a fairly clean, easily-metabolised alcohol. Fans of tomato juice love it.

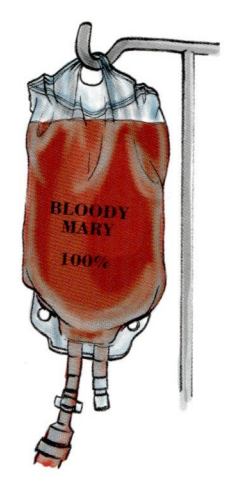

You can make it without the vodka, as a Virgin Mary, but really, what's the point of that?

Ingredients

- a big shot of vodka
- tomato juice – the best quality you can find
- a good dash of Worcestershire sauce
- a few drops of hot pepper sauce
- ground black pepper and salt to taste

Garnish

- A celery stick, but don't bother if you'll chuck it straight away.

Method

Mix well and serve over ice in a long glass.

Variations

This one can also be made with tequila – a Mexican Mary – if that's what you've got lying around, or gin – a Bloody Tonic – if you've only got that in.

PRAIRIE OYSTER

Look this one right in its beady yellow eye. It originally hails from America and contains some fairly magic ingredients your body really wants – yes even the egg bit. Add the vodka to show your liver you're not scared.

Ingredients

- a dash of olive oil
- a spoonful of tomato sauce or juice
- black pepper and salt to taste
- a dash of hot pepper sauce
- a dash of Worcestershire sauce
- a dash of lemon juice
- a shot of vodka
- a raw egg yolk

Garnish

The egg is quite enough, don't you think?

Method

Add a dash of olive oil to a long glass. Mix all the ingredients – except for the egg yolk – and pour them into the glass. Carefully tip the unbroken egg yolk in and serve. The key to this drink is to down it without breaking the yolk.

BANANA COW

Bananas contain magic things such as magnesium and potassium, which your body really needs right now. They also help replace sugars, and they taste nice, which makes this rum-packing drink an all round good thing for a hangover.

Ingredients

- a chopped up banana
- 2 tablespoons brown sugar
- a cup of milk
- a shot of rum
- ice

Garnish

Banana slices on a cocktail stick, or maybe a side order of chocolate.

Method

Whizz all the ingredients together in a blender and serve in a comfortingly chunky glass.

Variations

You can make a banana cow better – or worse depending on how you look at it – by adding cream, ice cream and crème de bananes.

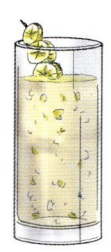

feeling BETTER?

The good news is that if you've made it this far you're probably going to be OK. But there's something you'd better do. It's time for you to make peace with your urinary tract; to give consideration to your pituitary gland; to revisit your cerebral cortex; to listen, nay to love, your poor, put-upon liver. On your next session though – and there will be a next time – put down that extra pint and spit out that last vodka cocktail and just think of how you'll feel the morning after.